Breakthrough Moments: 5 Step Formula for Getting Out of Your Own Way and Having the Life You Love

By

SUZIE EMILIOZZI

TABLE OF CONTENTS

ACKNOWLEDGEMENTS

To my wonderful healers, clients, friends, and family: you are magnificent teachers and wisdom-keepers. I am so grateful to you each day. It is my hope to honor you by sharing the insights, understandings, love, and compassion that they've so generously helped to cultivate within me.

A special thanks to my wonderful husband who offers unwavering support and love. I appreciate you with the depth and breadth that words cannot reach so I'll simply say I love you infinitely.

INTRODUCTION

I spent a long time experiencing what I didn't want while attempting to talk myself into being satisfied with it. I felt restless and frustrated, but I didn't know why. There was an incredible drive for success and career achievement. During this time, my career and roles in life told me who I was and what I should have. These roles also told me what I should enjoy and with whom I should spend my time. There were many rules, many "shoulds," and an extraordinary number of "have to's" in my day. There wasn't enough of anything to be truly and lastingly satisfied. There wasn't enough time or money. There wasn't enough fun or rest. There wasn't energy or well-being. There wasn't enough me. There wasn't enough love. There certainly wasn't enough success for it to feel meaningful. My health suffered. My attitude suffered. I felt depleted; yet, I pressed forward with more of the same. Surely, the next achievement, the new thing, or the change in venue would be "the" situation that uplifted, fulfilled, or inspired me.

Interestingly, if, at that time, someone had asked me if I were happy, I would have said yes. Now, I realize that I didn't know what happiness was for me. In fact, I didn't know who I was or what I wanted in life. I was anchored into what I thought I should be doing, feeling, and thinking rather than the delightful possibilities of me.

Now it's very clear: I was in my own way. In many ways, I held myself back from having the life that I desired. I created the stress and dissatisfaction that I experienced. I looked for completion and fulfillment outside of myself instead of accessing inner wisdom. It's also now clear that I needed to know and understand myself in a different way. I craved the enjoyment, freedom, peace, clarity, empowerment, and harmony that only comes from within the self.

This book outlines lessons learned through these years of self-discovery. It provides a conceptual framework for personal transformation. In a way, this book is like a cooking lesson; however, instead of teaching a single recipe, it teaches principles for cooking so you can make many meals rather than just one. This book suggests action steps for getting out of your own way so that you, too, can create what you want, enjoy the heck out of it, and love your life.

CORE CONCEPTS

Before moving forward, let's define breakthrough moments. Breakthrough moments are times of extraordinary change. These are times when mental, emotional, or other tangles that previously seemed like barriers fall away. In these moments, there is state of complete personal alignment, where an individual steps into the new, desired experience. You have probably already experienced breakthrough moments without realizing it. The five steps described in this book support self-reflection, empowerment, and personal growth that lead to more frequent breakthrough moments.

Underlying the 5-step approach are core concepts that give context to the work. Some are described below:

1. You have the inborn ability to heal, change, and grow. Every individual has these natural capabilities; it's simply inherent to all. In the past, these skills may have been under-utilized or under-directed but they exist nonetheless.

2. The stories of personal experience (as well as perspectives of self, the world, and others) are reflected within the body and life situations. For example, a person who often feels unsupported may find not only continued cases of being unsupported (or hung out to dry) but may also experience back or leg/knee/ankle issues.

3. You are not broken, and you do not need to be fixed. There may be some aspects of life or experience that have been limiting or unpleasant but, from a wider perspective, you are whole, complete, and magnificent.

4. The Universe is a loving place filled with wonderful possibilities.

5. You are loved completely, wholly, and boundlessly.

6. The Universe is always working for you, never against you.

7. Change can be easier and quicker than you may have ever guessed or imagined.

8. There are two fundamental approaches to change. The first is a process of excavation. It's about sorting through and resolving barriers/negative experiences. The other process is holding a helpful awareness. Helpful awareness puts emphasis onto what's already working in your favor. There is value in both approaches. As you're open to it, place more emphasis on helpful focus than on excavation. It's been my experience that helpful awareness moves us forward while automatically taking care of the barriers/negativity.

If your experience seems contrary to any of the core concepts, that's okay. As you move through the steps your focus, awareness, and perspectives may change so that you see your past differently.

A PERSONAL JOURNEY

In my early 20's, I developed a terrible case of Rheumatoid Arthritis. There I was in a new nursing career, with a new husband and a small child, and I was a mess. Everyday activities like brushing my teeth, getting into and out of the tub, tending to my son were all exhausting and challenging. There were times when I needed to be carried from place to place. As it progressed, I struggled to keep up with the pace of work and found myself on medical leave for periods of time. Although I had great and aggressive medical care, it just wasn't enough. I just wasn't getting significantly better. It was scary. I was depressed and anxious. Other health problems cropped up too. The financial fallout from that was also overwhelming. That's a lot of stress on a new marriage, and it fell apart. Outwardly I did my best to be a trooper. Inwardly, all I could do was focus on making it through the day. Everything was falling apart and yet I did my absolute best to talk myself into being okay. Clearly, I wasn't okay.

One day, something shifted. I received a gift certificate to my favorite spa. As I looked over the array of options, something caught my attention. It was an alternative/complementary healing system called BodyTalk. It sounded strange, and I didn't understand it at all but felt compelled to try it. That experience was a turning point in my life. Somehow I left feeling different. My mind couldn't make sense of it, but changes were apparent. Whatever "that" was, I knew that wanted more of it. The more I received, the more changes occurred in my body, perspectives, sense of well-being, relationships, and life.

Over time, I went into remission from the Rheumatoid Arthritis. The depression and anxiety resolved. My energy level improved. My overall health and well-being were improved dramatically. I started to know myself in a different way. I came to know that I wanted to help people create at least that level of extraordinary change in their lives. Those remarkable changes pointed me to a very personal path of growth and exploration. I studied not only BodyTalk but many other modalities and philosophies. Today, I am delighted to help others transform themselves and to create lives that are filled with all that's desired and meaningful to them.

STEP 1: PERMISSION

It may sound odd, but we often need permission from ourselves to move forward in some way. We are wonderfully complex beings and, as you've experienced, there are often inner conflicts about ideas, experiences, and personal goals. For our purposes, it is more helpful to focus on resolving internal conflicts rather than exploring and dissecting them.

Many internal conflicts are easily solved by giving oneself permission to heal, change, or move forward. Many conflicts relate to the following topics:

- Physical, mental, emotional, and spiritual healing
- Being present to and focused on the moment of now (rather than the past or future)
- Forgiveness and release/letting go
- Personal responsibility
- Being powerful/empowered
- Moving forward with one's own path regardless of what others may do

Conflicts involving other people, the world, and God/Source/Spirit/Universe are also common. Although it may sound strange, these too, may be resolved by giving oneself permission to heal, change, or move forward. Conflicts involving other people, the world, and spirituality (or religion) often relate to the following topics:

- The experience of being happy
- The experience of being healthy

- The experience of being sexually expressive
- The experience of being wealthy
- Being whole, loved, accepted by God, the world, or other people
- Being well-received by God, the world, or other people
- Being accepted by God, the world, or other people

Moving Forward Through Permission

There are as many ways to approach resolving this inner conflict as there are individuals. The process described here is intended for use at home, as a self-care measure. It may sound too easy, but it's easy enough. Before sharing the process, here are a few key concepts to keep in mind:

- The breath cycle plays a role in the healing and change process so it can be leveraged to begin the transformation process anytime, anywhere.
- The spoken word is powerful. There have been times when you've experienced the pain that has come with some words, and by contrast, the warmth, healing, and love that has come with other words. Harness this power by speaking permission phrases aloud.
- When using the spoken word (as a permission statement or during self-talk), it's very helpful to use, "I am" statements. The phrase, "I am" is accepted by the body-mind-spirit complex as fact. The practice of making helpful "I am" statements supports transformational change. Note that negative/unhelpful "I am" statements are also accepted as fact so changing the language you use about yourself can improve your experience.

- Personal choice is far more powerful than you may imagine. Choose to allow your choices *right now* to be the fuel for change in your life.

The Permissions Process

Begin with a rich, cleansing, and grounding breath. Choose to give yourself permission in one of the topics listed above (or for another topic that has been a known limitation for you). Make the statement (claim) aloud, using an "I give myself permission to…" or use another helpful "I am…" phrase. Breathe again, deeply and comfortably. You may find it useful to repeat the words, followed by a full breath, several times. Notice how you feel. Many people sense a difference immediately but have difficulty describing the change. Some people yawn, cry, sense heat or cold, feel a tingling sensation, or even detect a buildup and release of tension. Others notice little or nothing in response to the process. Whatever your experience, just choose to know that it is working for you.

Tip: Hydration is very helpful when making changes. Be sure to drink at least 8 glasses daily (unless there is a fluid restriction prescribed by your doctor).

As much as possible, apply the concept of permission to your life. Become aware of where you could benefit from giving yourself permission to either move forward or to let go.

Letting Go & Forgiveness

A question frequently asked is, "How do I let go? How do I forgive?" Within you, the ability and the experience of letting go/forgiveness already exist. While your thoughts and attention may have been drawn to pain, judgment, and disquiet, there is a place of openness, peace, and loving-kindness within you. This place is far greater than any of the difficulties you've experienced, so it's not a matter of working up to or into forgiveness or release. It's a matter of shining the light of your awareness on what already exists within you. This knowledge clears the path for greater empowerment to make inner changes of not only forgiveness and release but also opening to more love, possibilities, and opportunities.

Often the problems and hurts in life feel bigger than the self; it can feel like being at the mercy of the experience *du jour*. There is a sense of powerlessness, stuck-ness, victimization, lack of control, and more. In the thick of that experience, it is easy to forget the extraordinary nature of you. It's easy to forget that you're a powerful being, capable of great things. It's easy to forget that you are the director of your life. It is important to know that you can focus your attention and energy in such a way that things change – easily and quickly. Choose to remember (or now know) that you are extraordinary.

Shifting into the perspective of being the director of your experience is a way to recognize your authority. Remembering and claiming that inner state of power is transformative. It puts you in the position of influence over your life. Stated another way, recognizing/placing your focus on being the driver of your bus is transformational; it puts you in the position to make changes.

So how do you shine the light of awareness on that magnificent place within where forgiveness and letting go are inherent? It may sound too easy, but it's just easy enough. If you're sufficiently ready to go for it, then make the choice to forgive. Honestly, that can be all it takes: the choice to let go and move on.

If you think that you're not ready or you can't forgive/release, choose to be open to observing others who are. If you feel the person or situation is not worthy of forgiveness or release, then allow yourself to step further from the situation to take on the role of casual observer. You may find a new perspective from this view. In any situation involving a sense of stuckness or resistance, it is beneficial to shift your attention to openness. The statement, "I choose to be open" or "I choose to be open [to something that you are ready enough to explore/experience]" helps. As you embrace openness, there is a softening within that creates room for movement. Simply hold your focus around openness until you are willing to go there. Another strategy for letting go and forgiveness is to read books or watch movies about people who are forgiving, releasing, and changing. This works because people inherently relate to other people and also because humans communicate with themselves through symbols/metaphors, and stories.

Also consider this: at some point in your life, your feelings were hurt by someone who mattered to you. It may have been a minor infraction or something that hurt more deeply. Regardless, you found a way to forgive that person. Maybe it was because the relationship was important to you and you wanted to remain close. Maybe it was from necessity because not getting along would make a situation intolerable. Maybe the incident just didn't seem significant enough to hold close to the chest. Whatever it was, you found both a reason and a way to forgive and release. Anytime you feel it beneficial, you can meditate on the remembrance of such a time. As you do, it will remind you of your capacity for change, stability, and the steps for freedom. Ultimately, forgiveness and release is an act of compassion for oneself. Love yourself enough to let it go.

If you are open enough and ready enough, make a statement of your forgiveness aloud- either to yourself or another person. Then write it. Find multiple avenues of expression. You may sing it, draw it, paint it, sculpt it, or bake it- whatever is resonant with you. Know that as you forgive and release, you are loving yourself more completely. Breathe deeply and thoroughly. Find a way to celebrate yourself for having freed yourself from a burden. You deserve it!

STEP 2: SHIFT INTO A NEW PERSPECTIVE

It's easy to get stuck on a particular thought, idea, or view. Like that adage- it's hard to see the forest for all the trees. It becomes difficult to see something beyond what has already been experienced as well as beyond the current thoughts or feelings.

At times, it can even seem so overwhelming and bleak that it's a lot like being in a deep, dark hole with little hope of escape. Obviously that's not the optimal energy for experiencing more of what's desirable like joy, health, freedom & abundance. The question then arises, how is it done? How do you move from one perspective into another, even when you're deep in the thick of it? The short answer is: find a bridge.

The bridge between views takes different forms. It could look like getting clear about where you're going. It could look like merely stepping into new ways of thinking about yourself, others, or situations. It could look like embodying newness or taking new thoughts into your world. It could look like simply doing something differently that you have done it before. It can also look like allowing a storm of thoughts and emotions to pass.

From a physical standpoint, thoughts and feelings have been traced to a biochemical process. Further, they have been traced to a process where the brain uploads batches of memories (generally these are emotionally charged thoughts) to consciousness, at routine intervals. Consciousness only engages them for a short time – up to 30 seconds before a new batch is uploaded. You might think of it like a water mill. The brain is the wheel; memories are water. Bucket after bucket is filled with water; eventually the water is redeposited into the pool. Seeing the process as simply a wheel moving emotionally charged thoughts to and from awareness lessens their significance. There is little need to take them seriously. There is little need to believe or engage them. So, one bridge is to simply let any thoughts/emotions pass without engaging them. You can quietly observe – like watching the water move on the wheel, or you could imagine it like a thunderstorm. It shows up and then it passes. The only "action" is simply an observation. Simply hold the role of peaceful (non-engaging) observer until something helpful is experienced- a useful thought, constructive idea, a calm feeling.

Clarity

Generally speaking, it's valuable to know where you're going. If you want groceries, it's going to be more useful to go to a place that sells groceries rather than to a dentist office. Additionally, if you don't know where you're going then how will you know when you've arrived? Without knowing where you're going, it may be a long and arduous journey to get there; the arrival may feel like a matter of luck rather than intention. Do you see the inherent struggle in that? Notice the out-of-control, subject-to-the-whims of the universe energy there. Clearly that's not in alignment with a peaceful, empowered and confident perspective.

Maybe you already know exactly where you want to go. Maybe you just have a vague idea. Or...maybe you're clear very clear about what you don't want (poverty, pain, illness, sadness, guilt, stuckness, bad relationships). Most people can speak more readily about what they don't want rather than what they do want. Get clear about what's important to you. To jumpstart the process, below are questions for you to consider. Write your responses and keep them in a journal.

- What are your values? What matters to you? (See Appendix for list of commonly cited values)
- How do you want to be remembered when you're gone?

- Who do you want to be?
- Pick one or two of the values you hold most dear. How are you currently living/expressing what matters?
- If you're not fully expressing what matters most, what steps could you take to get there?
- What speaks to your heart? What is it that you desire more of, in your life? Is it freedom? Ease? Being more you? Vibrancy? Enjoyment? Excitement? There are no wrong answers here. Whatever brings you an experience of peace, relief, expansion, or joyful excitement is just right.
- Pick one or two of those experiences you most desire. What steps could you take to bring more of those experiences into your life?

Be well hydrated and be sure that your basic needs are met as you sit down to reflect on these questions. It will be more challenging to focus on the deeper questions if you're starving or exhausted. Also, that's a lot of soul-searching so you may need time to sit with a question before responding to it. Finally, take it question-by-question if needed. There's no need to rush or complete the worksheet in one sitting. Do what feels right to you.

Mindset

Helpful mindset creates a bridge too. This bridge is about taking on a paradigm of opportunities rather than bleakness. First, know that there are no wrong decisions in life. Some decisions align perfectly with your potential. Others do not. Either way, you're headed toward greater clarity and expansion. Either you will enjoy and appreciate the experience of the situation or you won't. If you don't, it's not the end of the world. It's simply an opportunity to get clearer about what it is that you desire to experience or create for yourself. Consider the non-enjoyment a redirection into what something that leads to joy.

Next, know that you can always choose again. Whatever has been, has been. Now is a new moment of incredible potential and empowered choice. You can choose what you want moving forward. Just keep choosing.

Another consideration of the mindset bridge is problems vs. opportunities. I used to work with someone who held the perspective that perceived problems are merely opportunities. He was really onto something! His catch phrase was that we worked in an "opportunity-rich environment"...and we did. There was always something coming up that created an opportunity for growth, change, improvement, teamwork, solutions, and creativity. The same goes for life. Everything that seems to challenge or provoke is an opportunity for greater clarity, understanding, awareness, solutions, change, expansion, empowerment, creativity, and love.

Taking it a step further, that which seems to bore, challenge, provoke, or incite a reaction is a blessing of exploration and awareness. This is really a form of internal communication. There is an emotional message that's calling for attention; it's calling for exploration or discovery. There's a call for attention to an experience of self or the world. When it occurs, it helps to take on the role of an internal scientist. What's this about? Stepping outside of judgment, what's calling for attention here? What would be helpful to understand, feel or know about this? Simply directing awareness can facilitate significant change.

Shifting Limiting Beliefs and Programming

The next bridge is releasing limiting beliefs and programming. Everyone has limiting beliefs. Personal experiences, perceptions, and misunderstanding lead to holding limiting ideas about oneself, others, and the world. Although all people are sovereign, whole, and complete beings, they are often affected by the beliefs and patterns of the human collective, families, and groups. Take a moment to consider the attitudes, beliefs, and ideas within your family that have helped you become the person you are today. Perhaps you were encouraged to further your education because those around you believed you were capable. Maybe honesty was highly valued so there were consequences for dishonest behavior. Extending this concept to the community, consider the beliefs, values, and practices of your community, friends, faith group, and work group have influenced you over the years. Additionally, energetic information like survival tactics, coping methods, beliefs, and various other patterns are often inherited from ancestors. You may recognize this by statements like, "he's just like his father" or "it runs in the family."

Regardless of their source (self-created, inherited, or tapped into), beliefs and patterns may be changed. It's all energy. It can move, transform, and transmute. Focused choice and direction are sufficient to move and change energy. Further, it's possible to adopt new, helpful beliefs. It's possible to release outdated beliefs and non-beliefs that hold back potential. It is possible, probable, and practical to change the energy and patterns within you.

You may be wondering how to shift beliefs, patterns, programming. One of the most helpful tools in transformation is awareness. Choose to become more aware of the thoughts that are running in the background. Thoughts are echoes of beliefs that are held about self, others, and the world. Become conscious of the negative and limiting thoughts as much as possible. Become aware of self-talk. As you notice them, take a moment to jot them down in a journal or log. Look for themes in your thoughts and self-talk. Look for the emotions related to those ideas (usually some version of fear or anger). As much as possible, strive to relate the idea to a belief.

As much as possible connect the thought to a belief. Here's an example of how it might play out: Jane felt insulted and hurt when Dan didn't greet her warmly. Jane's immediate conscious reaction is, "What's his problem? I don't deserve to be treated like that." She begins to notice agitation and annoyance. When focusing more, Jane is aware of an idea that "he always does this," as well as judgments about Dan. She also notices the presence of anger and then fear. When asking herself what's this about, an awareness of hurt is present and the thought, "nobody likes me." From there, Jane recalls an event from childhood when her peers rejected her. She notices the theme of not being good enough. She decides the underlying belief is, "I'm not good enough."

Jane now can shift the thinking. Here's what she does:

1. Takes a few comfortable, deep breaths to relax and regroup (after all, she's a little wound up)

2. She uses the breath of empowerment- full breath in and sigh/ hum on the exhale

3. She makes the choice and gives herself the direction to experience being "good enough."

4. She claims, "I am good enough. I choose to know that I am good enough. I choose to feel the goodness and lightness of being enough."

5. She uses another breath of empowerment and offers gratitude to herself for the opportunity to now be aware of what it feels like to embody "being enough."

It's as simple as that. Here are a few suggestions for keywords and themes to look for within your thoughts:

Always ~ Never ~ No-one ~ Everyone ~ Everything ~ Themes of all bad ~ Guilt ~ Should ~ Blame ~ If statements~ Can't ~ Won't ~ Helplessness ~ Judging ~ Labeling self or others ~ Not [good enough, from the right background, smart enough, pretty enough, look the right way, etc]

If you notice any of the keywords within your self-talk, thoughts, and conversations with others, then limiting ideas are present. Again, one approach is to choose more awareness and restate the idea in the true, helpful, and positive. You may find that you have several go-to negative, limiting thoughts. Many people do. It can take practice to retrain the thoughts. Focus on practicing the new ways of thinking rather than pressuring yourself to perform perfectly. There will be times when the practice is easy and comes naturally. Other times may require a little more effort or consistency.

You're not tied to who you have been in the past. Each moment is a new one. Each moment you are a new you, and you can embody a new thought, belief, and energy to carry forward. In each new moment, you can choose what to bring forward. In each new moment, you can choose a new experience- regardless of what your family or loved ones have done, thought, or have been. In each new moment, you can get to know yourself in a new way.

Avoiding Traps in Self-Examination

Many people get stuck in self-examination. Keep these tips in mind as you explore your thoughts and emotions:

- Withhold judgment about whatever you're noticing. Judging it doesn't help. Judging doesn't facilitate change. Judging the thought or the thinker only supports negative self-perceptions, a sense of being wrong or broken, it reinforces guilt, shame, anger, and fear.
- Even if you don't consciously agree with the content of the belief, accept it as something that has been represented within you. You

don't need to own it or feel sorry for it. You don't need to reject it either. Just notice it and choose to be present with the idea it represents.

- It is okay to feel whatever emotions come up as the awareness is present. If you find yourself rejecting the thought/belief, mentally chewing and dissecting it, or if you get caught up in the emotional charge of it, then it's probably not moving/shifting. Honestly, that's ok too. Please know that it's not critical to notice and change every negative thought or belief. You really can be a happy, satisfied, and fulfilled person while holding some limiting beliefs. It's totally okay to be human. That said, if it's a significant shift for you, it will continue to show up in some way until you get whatever change is helpful from it. You can never actually miss an opportunity.

STEP 3: EXPLORE THE POSSIBILITIES

Whether you have been in awareness of this, or not, you have already experienced breakthrough moments. Moments where you have completely stepped into a new situation and left behind any resistance, futility, imbalance, unhelpful patterns or judgments. Take a few minutes to recall past successes. Recall a few times when you had a goal or desire and took steps to achieve it. Recall a few times when a situation or item that you desired seemed to show up easily or unexpectedly. Remembering past successes is a useful habit that supports self-confidence, self-belief, and optimism. Positive self-regard and an optimistic approach open you up to greater possibilities.

Before delving deeply into the possibilities, let's take a look at a few common, limiting beliefs. Much like veils, limiting beliefs have a way of obscuring vision so that many possibilities go unnoticed or appear in a distorted way (that looks undesirable). The first common belief is an expression of helplessness: This is the way it's been so…this is the way it has to be. The next two beliefs reveal a sense of powerlessness:

- If this were meant for me (or if God wanted me to have it), then it would have shown up by now.
- I am supposed to/not supposed to [be, do, or have something]
- I don't know [what I want, who I am, what's expected of me, what's possible for me]

If these don't register with you consciously, that's fine. Often these or similar messages are held at a subconscious level.

In addition to limiting beliefs, attachment to a particular idea or outcome can get in the way of seeing and being open to new possibilities. In this context, attachment is an emotional charge around the outcome as well as an unhelpful mental expectation of what shall be.

Here's an example: Pretend that Fred wants to experience massive wealth, so he has an idea and builds a business around it. The business isn't going like he hoped- it's very slow to grow, and the idea he promotes isn't going anywhere. He's very emotionally invested in the success of this one idea, so he persists. The less successful he is, the harder he tries to sell others on the idea. The longer and harder he works, the more frustrated he gets. He just doesn't understand why it's this way. The more frustrated he gets, the worse the business does.

As an outsider, this situation is seen through a wider lens. Of course, *many* factors influence the success or failure of a company. Technical and management skills, strategic vision, timing, choosing the right market, ability to execute, having the right people in place all influence the success or failure of a business. The point here is that Fred is only open to experiencing success through this one channel: this one business idea. There could be a million ways that Fred achieves wealth. He's only focused on one. The opportunity here is to be open and flexible. Being open could lead Fred to change his business model or tweak the idea slightly. Being open could lead Fred to engage with people who could help him resolve a problem or find a new opportunity that leads to his desired success. Maybe if Fred were more honest with himself, he would become aware that what he wants is something else altogether.

Consider this: In what areas of your life could you be more open and flexible? What one or two steps could you take to help yourself?

With that in mind, begin to explore new possibilities. First, let your awareness softly land on an area of life that's important to you. It could be relationships (or one in particular), career, health, money/finances, creativity/self-expression, or something else. You're already well aware of how things have been going in that area so let's explore what could be experienced. Below is a list of questions to consider as you begin to explore your potential. It is helpful to make notes and review your responses often. You may find that your answers evolve over time, that's just fine. As they change, update them. Take a few moments to imagine what it would be like to have complete fulfillment in that area of life:

- How would it look?
- Who would be with you?
- How would you look?
- Who would you be?
- Who would you not be (anymore)?
- How does this change affect you?
- How does this experience change things in your relationships?
- How does this experience change things in your sense of purpose/meaning?
- What else is possible?
- What else is desired?

As you consider the possibilities, engage your imagination as much as possible. Engaging the senses is a wonderful way to stimulate the imagination. Draw, paint, color, paste photos/images, sculpt, write, sing, or use any other medium that appeals to you. The only limit to self-expression and achievement is limited imagination.

STEP 4: POWERFUL AUTHORITY

When you were growing up there may be have been confusing messages about how to get along in the world. Although well-intended, these messages may have said something like, " Don't stand out. You must fit in. You're dealt the cards you're dealt. Life is unfair. Life happens to you- get over it." These messages suggest hiding because the world is not safe or that you cannot be accepted as an influential person or if you're different than others. They also suggest that you're powerless. Life is, therefore, something to be handled or overcome rather than enjoyed and celebrated. They imply that life and unseen forces are pitted against you rather than loving and supporting you along the way. Additionally, you may have observed people who were in positions of authority or seemed powerful but were off-putting for some reason. Perhaps you saw unkind or unjust behaviors. Perhaps they conducted themselves in a harsh or judgmental way. If that's how power and authority have been witnessed, then it may be easy to conclude that power and authority are undesirable. All of these perspectives move you into a state of disempowerment. If you are aware of limiting attitudes and ideas related to power or authority, give yourself permission to be powerful (Step 1) and then find a bridge to shift them (Step 2).

Powerful Authority is about embodying that personal power that guides your life and experience. When engaging that personal power, you can more easily heal yourself and facilitate change whenever and wherever you desire. Key to the embodiment of personal authority is first knowing that it's possible (Step 3). Embodying that power requires accepting that you are that power. Ultimately, you are the director of your movie. You are the chef of the most magnificent meal that's imaginable. You are the boss of you. Claim it. Own it. Like anything else, owning power is a skill. It's something to be practiced, repeatedly.

As you own that power, you can literally direct yourself into a new experience. Applying concepts from the earlier steps:

Breathe deeply and center yourself.

As needed, claim permission.

Declare your power through an "I am" statement.

Choose the desired experience and give a direction to your entire being to *be* (embody) that which you desire most: wellness, happiness, freedom, etc.

Know that as you send that message to all of yourself, you are giving the direction to the infinite/Divine aspect of you to make it happen. The Infinite you exists beyond space and time. This aspect of you sees you completely, rather than the very limited and distorted view of the conscious mind. This Infinite you will always come through for you because you are completely loved, just as you are. As you engage with this aspect of yourself, you are further widening your awareness and opening to your potential.

If you encounter any resistance like doubt or negative self-talk, it's okay. This is merely an expression of fear or limitation. Breathe through it. If you are visually oriented, imagine the doubt/negativity as a small child that is crying for attention. Imagine picking up the child and attending to its needs. Hug and love the child. As you do, imagine it growing up to be a healthy, happy, well-adjusted adult. Visualize the adult wishing you well and walking away. By the way, the brain processes imagined scenarios the same as it does actual situations so visualization is a very helpful tool for making changes.

When life feels like a rough sea, it can be difficult to accept that you are, indeed, capable of smoothing the seas and motoring the boat to the desired shore. That, of course, is where a supportive perspective is helpful (Step 2). Do you see how these concepts weave together? Permission. Perspective. Possibilities. Powerful Authority. Each one feeds into and overlaps with the next, supporting personal choice, empowerment, genuine growth, and greater awareness.

If you have been waiting for a situation to fall into your lap, it may happen. Consider this: the greater expression of love for you may be to take a few (or even many) steps to achieve it. Perhaps the greater enjoyment comes from the unfolding of you that occurs while you are taking the steps to your most magnificent life (or that particular situation you desire).

If you're waiting for someone to change – for any reason – you may be waiting a lifetime. What if, instead, you chose another way to experience what you're looking for? If it's acceptance, that is something best received from within. What if you really and genuinely accepted yourself? If it's love or devotion…what if you loved yourself more and committed to being who you deserve to be? If it's an experience of partnership, what if you explored what it means to you to enjoy yourself and know/experience your potential? Take a moment to imagine what life could be if you stopped waiting or holding back. It's up to you to take the steps needed to love yourself into a new experience. Sometimes that may feel like work. That said, it's meaningful work and a wise investment because you are investing in yourself. You're worth it!

Make Room for Change

You have given yourself permission to change. You are practicing helpful perspectives. You are opening to new possibilities and claiming your power. Now, what? Give yourself the opportunity to experience the change. Make room for it in your life.

While some changes are very easy, others may require a little more attention so it helps to allow more wiggle room for self-care and exploration. With that in mind, give yourself a little extra time to take care of yourself. Simplify what's been complicated in your life. Reduce distractions that lead you away from what's important to you. Delegate, if possible. You are investing in yourself, for your best life and greatest happiness. Some things are best left for other people to manage so that you can focus where it matters.

At times, making room for change means letting go of something. Think of it like crossing monkey bars: one hand releases to grab the next bar. To fully reach the forward bar, you have to let go of the bar that's behind you. It is okay to let go of what hasn't been working or that no longer fits you.

Be kind by cutting yourself a break. Avoid taking yourself or the changes in your life too seriously. Allow the change to be a process of exploration. You're exploring what fits, what feels right, and what uplifts you. Some experiences will tickle you, others will not. Either way, you're following the path of breakthrough moments.

STEP 5: PURPOSEFUL ATTENTION

The final step for enjoying more Breakthrough Moments is holding purposeful attention. Focus and attention act like a magnet to create experiences that match the focus. At some point, you may have purchased a car. When you were thinking of buying that model of car, your attention was on it. As you went about your daily business, you probably noticed many cars of that model on the roads, in parking lots, and in garages. Your focus on that vehicle drew your attention to that car so you experienced it by seeing it around town. Additionally, you may have connected with a few people who own that vehicle and you may have driven one before you purchased it. That's how attention works: where you place it is what you experience. Use attention to your advantage by holding focus on what is meaningful and desirable to you.

Take time each day to feed the seed you want to grow and blossom. One approach is to meditate on the desired experience. Center yourself and then allow your imagination to draw an image of you as healthy, happy, full of vitality, and in the situations that matter to you. Engage the imagination as much as possible by imagining or pretending what it would be like to have that experience. Feel the emotions. Hear the compliments. Visualize yourself engaging with others in the desired situation. Bring in the senses of taste, touch, and smell if possible. A few minutes of this each day goes a long way to support helpful focus/ purposeful attention.

On the flip side, it is a short leap to imagine that attention to the unwanted could yield an unpleasant experience. If you're focused on what you don't want (i.e. money problems) then are you using attention in a way that supports what you do want? No, but avoid beating yourself up about it. What has been, has been. Now is a new moment. You are choosing again. Notice where there is a tendency to focus on the negative and then redirect that attention to the desired experience. Like most other skills, it takes practice to re-train the thoughts. Consider it mental exercise that's good for the heart.

Commitment is integral to Breakthrough Moments. As with any goal or desired experience, commitment is generally needed to create it. Imagine that you want to lose weight. You think about losing weight often. You know the steps required to get to your goal weight. Your thoughts are often on what you "should" do to lose the excess. Yet, there is inconsistent action taken so your weight stays the same. Although many excuses or explanations could be used here, an impartial view would reveal that full commitment to experiencing self as slim and healthy has been absent. Commitment says that you're serious about the experience you desire. Commitment invites opportunities that support your path to that experience.

Commitment is demonstrated through both attention (focus) and action. Begin to notice where your words, thoughts, and behaviors are incongruent. Consider what steps you could take to help them align. Explore what support you might need to consistently take steps toward your goal. Just to remove any pressure from the idea of consistency, conceptualize it as something that occurs more often than not. You don't have to get it right or be perfect; instead, just hold focus on what's desired and take the steps that are helpful more frequently.

BRINGING IT ALTOGETHER

Change is an inside job. Everything that's needed is already within you. Consider for a moment, a seed. Once planted, its inner power is released. All the potential of that tiny little seed transforms it into a beautiful, vibrant plant. With healing and change work, you're inviting your inner seed to activate and grow. You're setting up the nurturing environment that cultivates the seedling into a strong, healthy, vibrant being.

We are very creative beings so we can come up with many ways to stand between ourselves and our potential. We often hold ourselves back from experiencing the heart's desires by requiring permission from self, others, or God/Source/Spirit before we can move forward. Asking, "Why do I feel this way? Why is this so?" are not helpful questions for resolving inner conflict. Instead, claim permission. Claiming permission sets us free from old, binding chains and opens the door to change.

Letting go and forgiveness are areas where there tends to be a lot of struggle and strife. Holding on and withholding forgiveness serve only to feed old wounds, bitterness, and negativity. It's self-torture rather than punishment for another. Ultimately these are gifts of love to self. Choose to be ready enough to let go. Elect to be ready enough to forgive. Love yourself enough to set yourself free.

Adopt helpful perspectives. We experience ourselves and the world through the lenses of belief and past experience. Therefore, we can either be helped or hindered by the attitudes held about self, the world, and the perceived feedback from the world. Find an inner bridge of clarity, mindset, or otherwise to carry yourself from where you are to where you want to be. Boldly challenge limitations. If you find yourself with negative, harsh, judgmental thoughts. Stop and challenge them.

Choose to find a true, positive, helpful thought. Honestly, you've been through enough: have compassion for yourself. Compassion is an expression of love. Love is the universal solvent, the universal glue, the universal healer, and the universal fuel for growth.

We are only limited by the possibilities we can hold for ourselves. Begin to explore and open to greater possibilities. Connect with that powerful innate potential that's within you. Allow that potential to bring forth the delightful experiences you desire.

Each of us is the Captain of our own Ship, the CEO of our personal Organization, the Driver of our own Bus, and the Director of our own Movie. Often, life doesn't seem to teach us that. For a variety of reasons, there can be disempowerment. Accept that powerful inner authority so that you can direct your ship to go wherever you want. Moving into that place of power provides the opportunity to be you-to shine in whatever way is pleasing to you. It really gets all of you on board with creating the experiences that are desired. Embodying your personal power guides your life and experience so you can more easily heal yourself and facilitate change whenever and wherever you desire. Leverage the power of choice everywhere in your life. Let each new moment bring you a new opportunity, a new experience, a new you! You can choose again at any time.

Hold focus on what matters. Focus acts as a magnet, drawing experiences that resonate with our focus. Find ways to maintain focus on what you do want, rather than what you don't. Breakthrough moments can and do occur at any step, but this one is often the keystone.

SELF-CARE FOR TRANSFORMATIONAL TIMES

Self-care refers to activities and practices that support you both personally and professionally. Good self-care practices are essential for wellbeing and success. It can be easy to over-invest time, attention, and energy into other people, work, sports, or something else. Doing so compromises the ability to nourish and care for self. As a result, you feel drained, depleted and overwhelmed. It then seems like there's not enough time or energy to meet the demands. It might be helpful to think of self-care as putting on your oxygen mask. That must be done first, before helping other people. If you're depleted, it's very difficult to produce, to create, to love well, to be present, and to invest in what's important. Personal transformation requires generous amounts of energy (as well as a little time and focus). Unfortunately, self-care is often forgotten or ignored when it's most needed. It can be helpful to have a self-care plan in place while you're feeling good so that you can draw from that toolbox if you're ever too tired or too taxed to think clearly.

When creating a self-care plan, consider what you are *willing* to *commit* to doing *every day*. Keep it short, simple, and easily manageable. Helpful things to include in your self-care plan:

- Adequate sleep (at least 7 hours)
- Eating well and at routine intervals
- Regular exercise
- Mindfulness and meditative practice
- Time in nature (even 15 minutes in the back yard counts)
- Quiet time to relax, rejuvenate, contemplate

In case there is resistance to taking time for self-care, consider this: there are 1,440 minutes in a day. You can take 60-minutes for yourself. If needed, give yourself permission to take the time that's needed.

A template is provided to help you formulate your self-care plan. As you construct your plan, consider all the important factors of life: body, mind, spirit, emotions, relationships, work, faith community, and others of importance to you. Choose activities that are meaningful to you, ones that help you to feel good about yourself and your life. A downloadable worksheet is available at www.iamlivingjoy.com/self-care-plan.

Daily Actions for Self-Care

Plan for Routine Self-Care

Weekly Actions for Self-Care

Emergency Plan

The early warning signs that I need to activate my emergency plan are

As you create your emergency plan, consider your support system (personal, career-wise, and professional-level helpers).

Emergency Plan

Many people think of change like climbing a mountain. With any supportive gear and people necessary, steps are taken one-by-one to reach the goal at the summit. Instead, it may be more helpful to think of change as a winding path. Some areas of the track will be very clear, smooth, even, and easily visible. Other areas of the path may have an incline, be out of sight, or a little rough. Instead of focusing on the end result (the situation that you want to happen), strive to focus on the journey.

The path of personal transformation can be very easy and smooth. There is often a pleasant sense of physical wellbeing, as well as uplifted attitude and emotional states, and a sense that all is right in the world. Occasionally, it's less pleasant. As powerful inner change occurs, sometimes people find they feel intensely fatigued, have headaches, episodes of sleep disturbance, or other symptoms (these are often called "awakening symptoms"). If you begin to notice anything out-of-the-ordinary about yourself, give yourself a break from anything that's unnecessary in your life. If you're committed to many social activities, then it may be helpful to limit them for a few days. If it's possible to take a vacation day, then do. Use the time to rest and renew. Delegate whenever it's practical to do so. Strive to engage in activities that bring you more energy rather than drain you.

At times, it's helpful to seek support for blind spots. Everyone has blind spots: things that are difficult to see or accept about self or behavior. There is a lot of value in having support people who can offer feedback, different perspectives, or even scratch the itchy spot that's tough to reach.

Be open to getting help when needed. There may be times when you feel a little tired or stuck. There may be times you feel over-stretched, a little down, or depleted. If that's that the case, consider working with a change agent (e.g. healer, coach, or advisor). When deciding who might be a good fit for you as a partner in growth, it can be helpful keep these questions in mind:

- Do you see this person offering loving and non-judgmental support for your growth?
- Would this person be a champion/a cheerleader for your successes?
- Do you feel like you resonate/gel well with this person?
- Do you see this person holding expanded possibilities for you?
- Does this person encourage self-empowerment and personal choice?

If the answer is yes to those questions, then you have probably found a good match.

GETTING OUT OF A FUNK

Occasionally everyone experiences a funk. Maybe there was an unpleasant interaction with someone or stepped into a rabbit hole of disempowerment. It happens. A funk is a time of feeling "off" in some way. It can feel like agitation, restlessness, or emotionality. When you're not feeling like yourself, it is helpful to employ self-care to uplift, relax, and shift into a better state.

Breathwork

Stress affects the natural breath cycle. Ideally, everyone would breathe like babies: deep belly-moving breaths that gently rock the whole spine. With stress, there tends to be shallow breathing. Changing the breath is a quick and easy way to reduce stress and improve resiliency. Here are two options:

Left-nostril breathing: This is a modified version of a Yoga breathwork practice. With your eyes closed, try to "look" at your brow. If this is uncomfortable, focus on your forehead. Pinch your right nostril with your right thumb. Begin by breathing in and out slowly through the left nostril. When you have found a comfortable rhythm, start counting as you breathe in and out. Notice the breath count for inhalation and exhalation. Try to extend the count as long as is comfortable for you. Continue this practice for 3-5 minutes. When properly done, the breath will be seamless and comfortable (this can take practice).

Quick breaths: Close your eyes. Get comfortable. Then take 16 quick (approximately 3-count) breaths in and out. This practice is relaxing, refreshing, and energizing. You may notice a pleasant tingling sensation. If you experience a very light-headed feeling, it may be that you're breathing too fast.

Crystals & Minerals

Crystals and minerals provide subtle but powerful support. The natural energy patterns of the stones help to restore balance and harmony within an individual. Each type of stone offers something special. A few rocks are particularly helpful when feeling funky; these are described below:

Scolecite: This white colored stone provides a sense of security and safety while clearing negativity; it is useful when feeling uncomfortable or vulnerable around other people

Selenite: Selenite comes in many varieties; the one referenced here is white in color and appears striated. It is calming, soothing, and uplifting. This form of gypsum supports uplift while dispelling negativity; it also helps to reduce environmental influences.

Fuchsite: This seafoam or mint-green colored stone is often covered with gold mica. Fuchsite supports a balanced and healthy sense of responsibility. It aids in resiliency with emotional issues. It helps with issues involving relationships, as well as deeper healing, knowledge, and understanding.

Amazonite: This aqua colored stone supports emotional and mental balance. It soothes trauma and enhances a desirable connection between the heart and the mind. Amazonite enhances intuition, aids in accepting changes, and reduces feelings of overwhelm.

Black Tourmaline: Black tourmaline helps energy to move in the correct direction. It absorbs negativity and balances energy that runs near the skin (wei qi). It also transmutes environmental toxins (like electromagnetic energy from cell phones and emotional power surges from other people).

Lepidolite: This light purple form of mica provides calming support. It also enhances trust, self-love, and optimistic attitude. Lepidolite promotes personal renewal as well as reducing emotional disturbances like anxiety.

Seraphinite: This fern or forest green stone is uplifting and draws Divine energies into the subtle energy bodies. Seraphinite is great for issues of the heart like love, compassion, personal identity, and self-acceptance.

Do Something You Love

Stepping back from a situation for a little play time is often helpful to lift self out of a funky spell. Spend time in nature. Listen to the birds. Appreciate the sound of a wind chime. Pet a dog's belly. Watch a baby sleep. Hug a loved one. Create music or other artwork. Choose any activity that is uplifting to you.

Get Moving

Physical movement creates change. Take a walk or run. Clean the house. Weed the garden beds. Sort and clean a drawer or cabinet. Stretch or do yoga. If you're feeling stuck or extra-funky, strive for at least 20 minutes of activity past the point of sweating. From a Chinese Medicine perspective, this practice clears stagnant energy from the liver and, therefore, supports better emotional balance and detoxification.

Music

Sound has amazing healing properties and is an excellent way to move into a new state. Listen to music/sounds with a high vibration such as crystal singing bowls, Tibetan singing bowls, beautiful hymns or chants are quite therapeutic in this way. Any music that inspires you and lights up your heart or gives you a warm & fuzzy feeling will do the trick.

Focused Meditation

Meditation with a focus can be helpful in shifting into a new perspective and a more comfortable state of being. If you are new to meditation, a guided process may be necessary. One approach is to sit quietly with eyes closed, in a relaxed position. Select a word or phrase that describes the experience you desire (i.e. wholeness, peace, joy, compassion, freedom or something else). Take a few deep breaths in and out (or follow one of the breathwork techniques described above). Then allow your breath to fall into a natural rhythm. Focus on your word or phrase (a mantra). Intend to allow yourself to release any blocks or energies that are in the way of allowing that experience to occur naturally. Repeat the mantra until you feel better or until you begin to salivate. Salivating is a signal that your autonomic nervous system (the rest & digest function) has been activated- it means you are sufficiently relaxed, and your energy is shifting.

A free guided meditation is provided on www.IAMlivingjoy.com.

Prayer

Prayer is a wonderful way to shift the mind and emotions into a more balanced and comfortable state. Prayers of protection, grace, healing, peace, cleansing and otherwise can be very effective. The prayer can be as simple or as elaborate as you choose.

Water

If you're feeling funky, there's a good chance you're not well hydrated. Clean, pure water is an easy way to start feeling better. Since tap water is often poor quality, use filtered, purified water or high quality bottled water. At times, hot liquids are more appealing than cool liquids. If cool or room temperature water is unappealing, try drinking hot water with one or more of these additivities: fresh lemon, freshly grated ginger, fresh mint leaves, or cinnamon stick.

If you would like to give your water an extra boost, then pray over it. There are several effective ways to do this; here are just a few options:

- Write a word, intention, or prayer on a piece of paper. Set the water on the paper for a few seconds before drinking it.
- Hold the water and say a beautiful prayer of love, healing, or gratitude. Intend to infuse the healing energy received by the prayer into the water.
- Call upon a Saint, Angel or Ascended Master to infuse the water with the Light & Love of God or another high-vibrational energy.

Food

Fresh organic produce is another way to shift yourself out of a funk. Eat plenty of fresh fruits and vegetables; they provide not only nutrients and antioxidants but also uplifting energy. Give your food a boost through prayer or intention, as described above.

Aromatherapy

Uplifting essential oils and hydrosols effortlessly uplift mood, raise energy, and aid in shifting thoughts. Hydrosols are flower waters. These are byproducts of the essential oil distillation process; they may be sprayed into the air, on clothing or linens, or sprayed directly on the skin. Essential oils are very potent oils are extracted from plants. Many are extracted by steam (steam distilled), some are expressed/squeezed from fruit rinds (e.g. orange, lemon). Some flowers are too delicate for steam or yield too little oil from steam distillation so a chemical process is used to remove the oil. If possible, use only high-quality oils that are either expressed or steam extracted. At the end of the day, do you really want to breathe in more chemicals? Probably not.

Because essential oils are so potent, some oils are safe to apply to skin when mixed with a carrier oil (e.g. olive oil, almond oil) and others are not. If you have health problems, or you are pregnant, be sure to research essential oils before inhaling them or applying them to your skin. That said, most oils are generally regarded as safe. Placing a few drops of essential oil on a piece of paper is a quick vehicle for inhalation; gently fan the paper in the air to waft the aroma. Another practical approach is to place a few drops of oil in a diffuser; allow the diffuser to send tiny aroma particles in the air for your benefit and enjoyment.

Lavender: Lavender is relaxing, soothing, and balancing.

Frankincense: Frankincense supports peace and trust. It's deeply restorative.

Lemon Verbena and *Grapefruit*: These are uplifting oils.

Rosemary: Rosemary is clarifying; it helps with clearer thinking and changing habits.

Pennyroyal: Pennyroyal breaks up intense emotional and habitual energies.

Flower Essences

Flower essences are sometimes called flower remedies. They are designed to support the transformation of emotions, attitudes, and patterns of behavior that hinder the expression of the full human potential. Flower essences are generally created by placing the flower/plant in water for several hours. Because water is a conductive substance, the energetic imprint of the flower extends to the water. The flower/plant is then removed from the water and its imprint is "fixed" with a small amount of brandy. It may sound strange, but it works. Thousands of flower essences are available on the market. A few that work well for getting out of a funk are described here.

The standard use of flower essences is one-to-four drops orally (directly or added to water or tea), four times daily until relief is achieved.

I find that most people do well with twice daily. The support offered by this remedy is subtle but powerful. If you're very sensitive to energy, start with one or two drops at a time, once or twice daily. Notice how you feel and then adjust accordingly.

Rescue Remedy: This combination of multiple flower essences is available as a lozenge, liquid, or spray. Rescue Remedy is intended as a stress reliever. It works well to relieve tension, intensity, pressure, and other symptoms of stress.

Nootka Rose: Nootka Rose supports self-love and forgiveness. It aids in peace, love, and happiness. It balances subtle energies within and around the body.

Grape Hyacinth: Grape Hyacinth supports recovery from physical stress and trauma of accidents as well as promoting emotional recovery from past events. It aids in creating more space for change and wholeness.

Viburnum: Viburnum relieves self-doubt and insecurity. It also supports greater intuitive awareness so that inner guidance may be noticed and, therefore, followed more easily.

APPENDIX: VALUES

Abundance	Experience	Openness	Uniting
Acceptance	Experimentation	Orderliness	Uplifting
Accomplishment	Expression	Originality	Vitality
Accuracy	Facilitation	Participation	Winning
Acknowledgement	Family	Partnership	Wisdom
Adventure	Feelings	Passion	
Affection	Foster	Peace	
Artistry	Focus	Perfection	
Assistance/Help	Freedom	Performance	
Attainment	Fun	Persuasion	
Attraction	Governance	Planning	
Authenticity	Grace	Pleasure	
Authority	Greatness	Position	
Awakening	Growth	Power	
Awareness	Guidance	Preparedness	
Being	Harmony	Presence	
Being the best	Health	Productivity	
Beauty	Holiness	Provide	
Change	Honesty	Radiance	
Connection	Honor	Realization	
Collaboration	Humor	Recognition	
Community	Imagination	Relating	
Compassion	Improvement	Relationships	
Contribution	Independence	Respect	
Creation	Influence	Restraint	
Creativity	Information	Risk	

Danger	Inspiration	Romance	
Daring	Instruction	Seeing/Sensing	
Designing	Integration	Sensitivity	
Directness	Integrity	Sensuality	
Discernment	Invention	Service	
Education	Joy	Sexuality	
Effect/Impact	Kindness	Spirituality	
Elegance	Knowledge	Standards	
Enjoyment	Learning	Stimulating	
Enlightenment	Lightness	Strengthening	
Entertainment	Loyalty	Success	
Empathy	Mastery	Support	
Empowerment	Ministry	Style	
Encouragement	Modeling	Tasting	
Energy	Moving forward	Teaching	
Excellence	Nurturing	Touching	
Exhilaration	Observation	Trust	

29455688R00033

Made in the USA
Middletown, DE
20 February 2016